Her Teeth Are Stones
Judy Gaudet

The Acorn Press
Charlottetown
2005

Her Teeth Are Stones
ISBN 1-894838-19-X

Editing: Jane Ledwell
Cover image: Photo by David Helwig
Design: Matthew MacKay
Printing: Hignell Book Printing

The Acorn Press gratefully acknowledges the support of the Prince Edward
Island Council of the Arts and the Cultural Affairs Division of the PEI
Department of Community and Cultural Affairs.

Library and Archives Canada Cataloguing in Publication

Gaudet, Judy, 1949-
 Her teeth are stones / Judy Gaudet.

Poems.
ISBN 1-894838-19-X

 I. Title.

PS8563.A823H47 2005   C811'.6   C2005-906223-1

The Acorn Press
P.O. Box 22024
Charlottetown, Prince Edward Island
Canada C1A 9J2
www.acornpresscanada.com

For David, my centre

Contents

HER TEETH ARE STONES

Photographs 9
The centre of belief is love 10
Daydreaming 11
Queen St 12
Wallace Hall 13
At the Public Gardens 14
Heron 15
Bouquet 16
Invocation at Wolfe Island 17
Lines on a page 18
When after war with children 20
Every space a door 21
Clare 22
Spiders 24
Earwigs 25
Enough 26
Settlements 27
The sighted man takes flight from eternity 29
The bus stopped there 30
In a wild garden 32
Paris 33
My daughter in summer 36
Delivery 37
Poems, you say, 39
Tu Fu Speaks 42
Ancestors 43
Family tree 44
The aunts 46
Millie 47
Random gifts 55
The Word 56
The dying of trees 57
November Gregorian 58
Random words — *pax* 59
Aura 60
The path 62

Photographs

The too vivid flowers — gardens of clothing —
cloak the kind hearts of my lost ones.
Where, in scant and gaudy pictures,
is the way the air moved the raspberry canes,
or the sudden joy when they came to camp
dressed in flowers and I was no longer alien?

Every moment we live is temporary, but real
as memories and photographs can't be,
full of delicate movement. A monarch
butterfly skims through the raspberry canes.
Outside time it's all pictures of doubtful validity,
irretrievably lost. But we're inside it.

Here we are. The wind rustles the raspberry leaves.
We take the berries in for breakfast.
If our dresses are covered in flowers
we laugh. We like them.
Don't look on from outside
but come inside. Beauty is infinite here.

The centre of belief is love

A ruby-throated hummingbird
comes almost every day to the delphiniums
outside my window, hovers there,
unfrightened as I'm unstartled.
We accept each other as regulars,
but Joe saw one once in Barbados,
its suddenness left him "soppy
with a sense of wonder, blessed."

In the cut-down woods behind our house
wood has been left chaotic on the ground
but Linda has stared astonished at the snags.
"Look at them, on every branch, all up and down."
Birds. The perfect place for birds.

And underneath, David discovered
one day he got lost, acres of raspberries.
They're clean above and below, free
of bugs and mildew and snakes, even
standing on old trunks, tangled and brambled,
it's clean high and low, the sun shines,
the world is sweet where David walks.

Daydreaming

Life goes by fast when you're having fun
I say, and my daughter says, you didn't notice
because you were daydreaming.
And perhaps I was, about the girl who read
a headline in the checkout counter about famous
musicians speaking to the living and creating
through them, and letting the music of Chopin
invent itself through her fingers, about a streetcorner
where she felt clever about choosing the right lights
and strangers or angels smiled approval, a girl
who imagined aliens approved; it's not a bad species,
look at the young, how pure and passionate.

An odd girl surely, and children are odd yet.
Boys who knock their friends to the floor
and wish they could have farted too are shocked
to hear of slavery; they would have sided
with the right; and there was a woman
who would have sided with the right under Mount Doom,
who would have brought light on a jungle path,
who was bad tempered and had sore feet in this world,

a world where one's daughter is 40, one's son 50,
where you've hardly noticed time pass and yet
have worlds and worlds, lives and lives, other people
you once were, I suppose their lives count too
when you add up your own; I've been all this and this
but how does it add up, what's the sum, who is smiling
approval?
          As you sort out the negative file, you see
you've known stone flowerpots and still lakes, beaches
of white snow against blue sea, flowers and sun,
and dim, intense falls like these: been, seen, recorded.

They are a nice species surely, to wish for, keen,
be keen, as long as the sun rises, no matter
whether buildings, or old ways, or the economy
falls, and believe, life is not long, not long enough.

Queen St

Here's the answer to the question about where
the birds go when it rains or snows
or the slush in between today when I hear them
in a cedar bush in front of the library on Queen St.

They're all there, twittering and whistling their songs
giving the bush a voice flashing sonar light when
I walk up to it and peer in under the branches.
They're all there and cock their eyes at me,
take a moment's silence to look me over,
a mortal eye looking in under their cover to find
the sound and secret of mystery.

Where have they all gone? Kate asked when she was an old
woman sitting in her rocking chair,
all the herons and swallows, all the sparrows,
you never hear a bird.

                    Maybe they're not all gone
as we fear, maybe they're hidden under branches
in bushes on Queen St, waiting for us to walk on by
so they can go back to their magic of making bushes sing.

When I was a kid on my way to the library
the clouds made paths in the sky, roads,
with the gateway just above.
And now this!

Wallace Hall

                then wait,
a flutter in the crabapple blossoms
& the pianist walks longfingered away
with a cigarette, then
the still of no chords on the ledge, & drops
of the hose spray the red geraniums,
                                      wait
while the pink blossoms make a rustling in the tree
& drop off into sparrows

At the Public Gardens

Starlings startle the waters
in their mania of splashing
while the turtle's head never moves.

For him the impressions of a minute
take hours to bathe in.
At the end of the day he has been washed in eternity.

Just the sun on his head
the cool water on his feet
while the starlings have tickled every feather & flown off.

Heron

When ice breaks up along the shore
black-backed gulls cry out like geese
honking back into spring as a tease,
waves lap, the heron stands and strides out or

watches from the corner of his eye
to see a fish swim near, or the light of sea or air,
or me stalking with a camera, fair
game to want a picture, no injury

intended, and he accepts it that way,
stands, stalks, while the water laps, stretches
head out, makes a *u* of his neck, catches
me coming closer and watching, then, hey,

off he flies, from *s* to horizontal *i*, glides
against the sea and rocky shore, past
what the winter storms have cast
up, trees they've thrown down, rides

all change and threat to the one quiet
place that is his own, still water by the rock's
edge, another spring, ice gone out, walks
his long walk, and for short danger, short flight.

Bouquet

the crows call
and fly back to the woods

the sun brushes on my arms
wind rushes the leaves on the linden
to make a song
and a chickadee sings
"sweet weather"
while I reach down among thyme
and mint and lavender
and roses
that pierce me
so I sing, "Ouch"

a succubus has jumped on Joe
he says and replaced his spirit
with her own
chemo brought her
and made his flesh foreign to him
made things smell bad

here is a bouquet of these things
my hands went down among

get out awhile, evil jinn,
leave Joe with us to love the day

the crows are calling out
flying back into the woods
for one of their own

Invocation at Wolfe Island

"But still I know that life is for delight."
— D. H. Lawrence

from inside this blue room I hear
the boys leaping from the ferry dock,
the wind in the leaves over the lake, I see
shadows from the tree moving over stones,
over the tinkling key of a boat's mast,
a white butterfly's passing

an old book of poetry invokes
the spirit of invoking,
after Lawrence wrote, after Tom read,
after their transient mutual delight,
oh shadows of dark wind
over the light haze of water!
oh crow's voice shushed by the tree's command!
oh wishing leaves, whoosh, buzz
of flies coming through open doors
and going out again!
oh life that goes on, carrying so much,
uncountable in the time that brings it —
life coming in on a breeze,
on a wave, on a voice over water,
on a mosquito's wing, a swallow's pursuit,
life looking out and looking in,
here is a soft stirring of spirit, response,
repose, shush, shush,
here are the million gifts of this single now.

Lines on a page

On my calendar Escher stands birds behind lines of, what, a fence,
    some kinds of wires you wouldn't expect to find
      on the fifth day of creation
and the coincidence buzzes at the back of my mind as the images
    of the space shuttle coming to Earth then exploding
      toward the Earth, bits flaring in gleaming shadows behind it,
crosses lines of electric wires on the tv, inducing a tenderness
    somewhere that coincidence is proof of God,
      pattern makes sense, all things work together,
and oddly these deaths bring out a kind of goodness we don't often follow
    on tv, astronauts and their families coming from that ordinary
      decent world that so rarely makes the news
and so we see the sister of one man who says, This
    is what he always wanted to do and he succeeded,
      for all the injustice that happens every day, he won,
and the brother of another says, He was so happy in space
    that he said he didn't want to come back to Earth,
      and now he hasn't, he's stayed out there.
One man is Black and stands for Opportunity in a land where racism
    and inequality are severe,
another is Israeli and his unwordly goodness is writ large
    on tv screens where his country's
      violence so often now is shown,
Joe is led to comment on the nature of Death, why we should care
    about the loss of seven
      when every day so many millions die,
and led to justify his love of Israel by saying, War is part
    of our animal heritage, a natural way
      to keep the population down
when in the normal course of history or Nation building,
    and stops just short of saying Death
      doesn't matter, Life is cheap,
though his voice tells that he's heartbroken that suffering
    exists in nature and why does God allow this?
      His theory lets death but not suffering be natural,
and why should we care for this suffering, loss, fact,
    when biological imperative is being served?

But we do, we do.
This is a morning I woke up happy on, when I walked and read
        and the chickadees flew down to the feeder, when trees
        shed ice sheaths like bells and mists made snowy hills magic.
This is a day after a day of despair hearing we are buying
        into the economics of making war machinery,
        an economics driving the self-righteous
rhetoric that will pit Israel against its helpless neighbours, the US
        against the children of Iraq, a day on which seven
        men and women burnt up hurtling toward Earth from Space
and didn't undo but enhanced the value of the lives they'd lived,
        and their President, so free
        with others' lives, beautifully eulogized theirs,
a day when Joe, neither a bad man nor a good, justifies Israel's
        wars against a people it has no
        use for and feels it has a right to remove,
but, tangled in animal equivalences, nevertheless finds
        his voice breaking when he speaks
        of these few real, spectacular, and symbolic deaths.

When after war with children

When after war with children some appear
their courtesy reminds me they are not just made for death.
The cheerful boys ask after books of war oh yes they know
the inventor of the u-boat, and the tank, and missiles,
admire strategies, hear with glee about the evil men whose love
of death and power made millions die, powerlessly. One wants to believe
in youth, and that these are innocent, that their enthusiasm
has nothing to do with the suffering and death it really was.
One thinks with cynicism, They'll find out some day, they're born
for cannon fodder, in suffering and death they won't swagger gladly
over the doings of vicious men. Or maybe they'll become vicious men.
But now there's no satisfaction in these projections, they're still children,
they want war like they want hockey, or a fast car, or an adventure,
they love evil men like they love achievement, more, it's more obvious.
These are children, who know nothing of evil except the possibility.
It's the largeness, the largeness of cruelty, destruction, forces massed,
annihilation, they are children and they love the power to annihilate,
to win, My side wins! Oh did you see Bobby take down Chris at recess?
Oh Hitler! He was a really evil man! I try to think it's not admiration
in Daniel's voice. Oh I don't want anything to do with children
and their eagerness but the next day they are keen on other things,
it's their way to be enthusiastic and after you have warred with children
they no longer want to play war, may feel quiet and safe that day
and want to be quiet and safe and to play some other game,
and I hope there's something left to play.

Every space a door

This peaceful room, composed
of plants, and of cats, and of wood
and white furnishings
supplants the bone-weariness
the frenzy, the energy of a day
in which news of a young boy's death

by his own hand
gun to mouth

was only part of my discovery
of the world of young boys.

Here, his death is as much
and no more mine than the change
that's coming over the trees outside,
the dusk that's coming over the day.

These peaceful flowers and I
sit by the windowsill

and while not all of life is windows
still, it may be better to avoid the drop
from three storeys' height
than to think every space a door.

Clare

her fragility goes past her bent back,
her faith in green tea, her wish
to live alone with cats on a forest path,

all her past is fragile, and her faith,
and the way she mourns the young
cat's disappearance or nurses the old's

illness, her back broken twice falling
off roofs, the Sadhu with his small importunate
penis pursuing her, searching for a night's rest

and her fall, smashing her face on the wall
she hit first, and her heels as they jammed
the earth, and the lumbar bones that folded,

the taxi ride over rough ground, the rattling
they gave her to X-ray her, then moving here
to her house with its oddities,

her delight in the single path she stamps
on the ground, and the crumbling tunnel
under the tracks she persuaded her cat to follow

her into, crawling on her belly miles
from her isolated house, the way
her back mended when she so easily

might have died, the way her old cat,
kept alive by expensive medicines,
survived, the new relationship

the young cat's disappearance opened
up for them, the way she only wants
to write, and live, and live long

enough to let her age catch up to her back's
age, and just work enough to pay
her cat's bills and the cost of green tea

tablets, to prove life has some holy and good
pleasures, the yama and niyama the celibate
monks forgot, her innocence as she speaks

of all these things that are and were and
may be, and how her heart beat so wildly
when the male monkey leapt on her breast

and clung to her thin dress and bared
his teeth, snarling, and how frightened she was
he would bite her breasts, makes her seem

so fragile sitting by our fire, thinking
of what route is surest to get through the storm
back to her own house, her own old cat

Spiders

Every space between bushes and trees,
between the playhouse and a poplar,
between the apple and the pear,
between a spruce and a morning-glory-covered lupin,
every tall spire where there were delphinium
or phlox or sunflowers or tiger lilies is roped off.

When you stand beside the garden, tree or playhouse
where the spider reigns it huddles up alertly.
These spiders' webs are not gossamer things but sturdy nets.
They themselves are large and hairy, like pets,
not something hidden away but declaring their rights.

I don't doubt the spider's right to rule in my garden.
In fall these spiders lace it all, and I simply stay out.
I don't lean into the garden to trim back stems,
or walk in the wild places between trees in the ravine.
I check openings between things in my yard
and finding them occupied I go around.

You'd think perhaps some kind of bird
would have a feast in my garden getting ready for winter,
and perhaps that will happen before frost comes.
But meantime spiders in dozens and hundreds
reign supreme, at least in my garden,
where I hope they remove the more timid insects,
and I respect them, fear them.

Earwigs

The odd one stands lazily on the butterdish,
on the curtain rod, on the window sash,
making a little dodge just before I
squish it with a paper towel; I can stand that.

They scurry quickly, frantic, legs spinning under
them to get away when I open a bag they're in
or lift up a plant they've made a nest in the roots of,
hurrying away as if caught in a hundred indiscretions.

I would like to be a pacifist on the Earth, find balance,
blot a few with hoeing, hand killing, careful ways.
I don't want to grab the can of house and garden spray
and cover the gaillardia with it; but I do.

In the evening they hurry up the side of the house,
pour through the windows as if they're late for a lynching,
set up councils, writhe on the floor. They leave their meeting
place tidy in the morning; but I call the Pest Control.

Enough

"But enough of death — it's life that matters,"
says Virginia Woolf, when suddenly freed,
unchained, you examine the forces driving
you violently or with a hidden laugh
away from the past that follows you there
to France, say, and is in your head with you,
you shaking it off, or enjoying it perhaps,
as if you can leave home behind
and bring it too, or else, what would
show you'd been this path at all, your little
congeries of atoms, your little self carrying
not only your life but all you see, the world,
how that is, to what will be?

Settlements

I

Against antagonist winds the wooden ship's straining sails
find safe harbour, channelled willy-nilly broadside
in the red sands of the Island.
                              Leaving the turbulent hull of it
the soldier and his wife and four children, having maintained
good characters home in Scotland, find themselves landed
in a red and blue cove of something they will not leave in this life,
and young Margaret, with a face like a noble savage, marries up the hill
a bearded man like a patriarch, their kingdom looking down over it
follows generations, their daughters long afterwards picnicking
on fallen branches over the long blue bay at last empty of ships,
the waves grass.
                    And Mary, proud as a Queen and twice as regal,
comes up the hill on her way home from the Boston states, between
stints as a servant, to be gathered in the many arms of her family,
old Aunt Sarah throwing her great grandsons into the air, men
who cut paths through soil, through ice, despite what spurts of frost
prevent the plough, who open their doors for the wanderer,
but stay home themselves, whose settlement is as enduring
as that of bearded men can be where the blue waters run red with sand.

II

Never driven out so much as leaping in front of defeat
they landed awhile in a Scotland of the backroads,
dark hair and eyes peering earnest in hope, clean in youth,
stalwart in age, then throwing off their best suits, taking up
their fishing lines and searching the deep pools by the mill,
bringing home trout for summer dinners with sly smiles,
fishing the earth for potatoes, roots and green tips, food
to feed their journey up and away, their eyes on the road ahead.

The sighted man takes flight from eternity

When the sighted man
with half his eyes closed
and the others blue, grey, heron,
saw the Island, he was struck
with the softness of it, and said
it was a lyric land, as if a poem.

He said there are two Islands:
one sleeps and one faces the sea,
and the sea broods;
                    even
with his shut eyes and his blue
eyes he could see the land
ploughed, green, fallow, standing
orderly in spruce and wild cherry;

even with his grey eyes and his shut eyes
he could see the lapping sea
laughing inland from eternity;

but with his heron eyes, he saw
what made him leave, saw
the tranquility of years, saw
the bright peace of colours
more brilliant than life
more beautiful than what is real
and missed his fears, his heron eyes
saw, and tempted his wings away.

The bus stopped there

In a crisp Montreal day in fall, lines of children
form around a square to load onto buses, the statues
and water fountains left to pigeons.
We are part of the metropolis now, lined up
with men and women who work in tall buildings
downtown, shop, their faces impassive on bus seats,
parcels on their laps, their hands hanging
onto overhead lines, or reaching for bells
to disembark in windy canyons under glass.
We're among them, coming in from everywhere
through the city, to our own brick worlds,
our own uniforms and books and lives.

There's something about the cold and the smell
of the square, around the edges of which the buses took on
their various passengers, that means business even now,
so long after I outgrew my uniform, left that place, dig
tenderly in what was, as hard to find as if Then
was not Now, as solid as to block off all alternative.

The business of buildings, bus stops, certain people known
and so many thousands unknown, later emerged
as having lived just there, at that posh corner, a writer,
there, just up the hill from me, a customs officer and later
blind man who borrowed books from my library and whose
dog had a library card also, there, by the park, in stones
unimaginably well laid down, girls with wool skirts and sweaters.

My buildings: one church with stone columns in a Greek style,
one red brick library and observatory (with flowers) in a park,
one yellow brick school in the shape of a U opposite a University,
the University itself on the mountain, several large stone stores,
the soul of what it's like here, now vacant or rearranged,
one market under a hill (centred with pork roasts and surrounded
with bags of tomatoes and corn), one flat upstairs, one bank,
one Forum emptying of a circus, two hospitals on a corner,
a few glass towers, one Central Station with trains underneath

emerging to bridges and home in summertime, and after a bit,
one subway system, one island with a world's fair on it,
one Art gallery, one walled monastery, one bus station at which
to set off to college on windy wintry days in short skirts,
one mountain up which to walk a dog on jungle paths, one lake,
one stone wall overlooking a city, two great parks, this was Now,
this was Here and here and Ever Shall Be, This is It, now
try to remember how it all was, and its present hip dressing
of graffiti makes another Now, certainty is this way, crêpes
with fruit from all round the world, people in sidewalk cafés.

In a wild garden

in a wild garden
far from the streets of Marseilles
we lie on Earth's bones

her teeth are small stones
perfect and white in sunshine
we eat our sandwich

alone on rock cliffs
we sit on thyme and iris
hear the seagulls cry

disused armouries
guard ships that are not passing
and white birds that are

the cries of voices
wheeling over the blue sea
they own these islands

Paris

in PEI a white whipping
over white hills past white houses
keeps us indoors heating our blood,
the sounds: vertical gusts from the basement,
horizontal gusts past three pale windows

we look down on the clouds,
a free sort of wool weaving,
sometimes skip on the points
of their updrafts,
we descend from infinity
to a distinct strip of runway
still in the clouds,
run for miles in obscurity
except for occasional startling
highways running beneath us,
our wingtips just avoiding
bumping into the temporal

when we open the windows
for our brie on the ledge
— a just cool pantry —
we hear a piano playing,
a canary set out to sing,
a voice nagging a bit shrilly,
these evidences of ordinary life
welcome among the cobblestones,
the winking green men,
scurrying small cars,
children on donkeys,
sunny benches,
stone men and horses,
pigeons sitting down for tea
in the laps of Bishops

a cathedral is a darkness,
a collaboration between craftsmen and sun

held up for shining through
by monumental feet and hands
deliberately dimmed,
the stones, pillars and arches,
its beautiful and interior bones,
are in service to a prism, the eye
through which enters the great pageant, Art

false art: wet feet on a rainy day,
an overeager man fronting a magazine
or a film company, so false you can't tell
exactly the source or sum of the falseness,
an overpriced gift and a scornful seller
who, gathering it all up, smashes it
and then offers a discount on the ruins

true art: ghosts on palatial steps,
stone archways where Mesopotamian lions sit,
the ancient bearded man with a freshly killed goat,
and in me a flash of fresher anger:
the seat of civilization razed
to make way for a smarter set of truths,
oh how cleanly the oldest stones sit together
but after miles of it I have such sore feet
and who can love all I have loved and seen?
the poster reads, *"je fait rire le monde
et le monde me fait pleurer"*

on a long upward flight
of stone steps I begin
to turn to stone from the feet up,
legs heavy as marble
lift more slowly over each block,
along pebbly quays
I avoid the edge, as,
if I joined the ducks
I would not float,

but sitting warming in the sun
I'm glad my head is still my own
to see the lovers *aux rives de la Seine,*
laughing friends spread tablecloths,
eat, drink wine and speak in every language
while the leaves and blossoms
open around us all
in the soft Parisian air

sitting on a plane,
the land slowly unfolding beneath me,
may be a bit like looking down
from a quite high mountain
it's hard to say just how high a mountain,
one that makes the world seem like a map,
coastlines, islands, *le grand fleuve,*
even the small Port au Persil
behind its island is shown
by the way the road runs down to the shore
and then back up, the blue Saguenay behind
while we fly serenely overland unrolling
hills, lakes and forests, and on them
man's careful markings, roads,
make a benign statement on his behalf

from on this quite high mountain this question:
if God didn't want anything from you
and you nothing from God, would you still love Him?

the snow has melted from the front step
I read David's poems, type out my own
we look at pictures on the wide screen
add more windows to our rooms

My daughter in summer

here is the body caught perfectly
in flight from dock to river
that day, and, today again,
those cells' descendants transcribe
almost exactly the same event,
the body now, a bathing suit,
the feet leaving the ground behind,
the sun on flesh, a breeze on
warmed skin, approaching the very blue
surface, the immersion of the head,
the spray on legs and feet,
all plunged in smooth clear water,
the sensations of the present
in continual brief explosions of Now,
Life, life, life, the sand on the soles
of feet, water dropping and running
from hair, the sun warming lifted arms,
the air licking the skin dry, the teeth's
smile, the voice calling out, laughing,
the answer.

Delivery

1977:

I dreamed I set 6 separate fires
and hid them in a bag in Eaton's.
When I woke a liquid ran down my legs,
then nothing, if blood is nothing:
no fire department, no flood control,
just wait, like much of being pregnant
I thought, just a matter of waiting.
Others came, moaned, screamed,
delivered up a child, but for me, a mild
cramp, and a backrub, and just wait.

Sintoxin entered my blood, 6 fires
burning, and the paper bag flamed.
The next step, breathing, puffed like a bellows,
louder than any voices in the room
where my body lay, effaced, contracted,
did its work, until, now, ride the trolley,
stare at the ceiling, place your legs in stirrups,
ride this tremendous excavation of self,
freeze in terror, what you will, Now is the time!
for a little cry, a waving hand, the arrival of another.

1979:

What I know will soon prove somebody arriving
presses on the nerves at the tops of my legs,
catches me up, doubles me over, pitches me
into alarm that takes me, waiting alone, up
a high spiral of terror. Women have babies
I tell myself, you've had one. But they also die.
Though I hope to meet death calmly someday
not today, no, not now! In the dark my blood rises.
Not yet! God begins to bargain. Live, then!
Alarmed, nurses run in, medicate.

The next morning halcyon aftermath. Mildly,
contractions begin, we chat, between cool breaths,
not suspecting the time, until we are all amazed,
I start to push, am wheeled across, deliver.
My own doctor is absent, a woman doctor
does all that's needed with gentle efficiency
and looks at me with an approval I return. God keeps
his bargains I tell myself, keep yours. The baby,
large and healthy, looks at me with a calm interest.

"Are you coming home tonight, Mommy?"
her sister asks. "No, not tonight."

1984:

Whatever stubborn thought has required another
I am treated to tests and bloodletting, ageing
parturition. I cry when it's late, have not babies
but amniocentesis and ultrasound.
No amniotic fluid, an appointment for next day,
a drip, but they've divided the ocean into parts
too large, each drop is a tsunami, under which
I swirl, falter, cannot break surface, can't speak.
"Moderate pains" say nurses sailing overhead,
heartbeats flashing on a monitor, doctors peering, ask,
"Caesarian? Can she speak? " IV, Cervix Dilate,
Amniotic Fluid, Heart Graph, Dramatic Dip,
Swallowed Meconium, Cord Wrapped? Come Up!
Stop Hiding Out Underneath! "She's answering.
Let her try." I swim up, perhaps have been
too deep. Push! Push! Fraught with danger but
we arrive, flotsam ashore, anchored with IVs, land.

"One minute I'm the baby sister, the next the grown-up
sister," my daughter tells her aunt. And the oldest girl,
excited, pauses a moment in learning the steps in her dance.

Poems, you say,

                        small
messages, cryptic, coded,
undirected, or meant for God
or the dead,
                        or some
other version of self far
in the past or future,
here I am being human,
                        God,
this is what it's like
to secretly spend
your dancing money on sweets
be an immigrant to your own
country, live in a city you would not
visit,
        stand on a step you did not
once want to admit to living above,
live above yourself looking down
as you do, God, on all the hats judging the size
of soul they house.

                        Mary
I named my daughter for you because
when I was five and you
                        were ninety-five
you found me hiding under the bed.
You had such a hatsize and then
                                    in pictures
such hats, and I try to put them together,
the pictures, the clothes, the souls, to make one
life, but only God can, and where he is you are too.

Washing the dishes this morning I discovered
the little girl I'd been, sweet and shy,
had grown to carry the weight of family,
all the time saying,
                        gender has nothing to do

with hat size, I'm just a person,
and am surprised at my surprise
            that I've lived a woman's life.

                            All those pictures
of hats before they went out of style covering the heads
of my past,
            they all loved good hats,
                                    their souls
matched, I think,
            what do you think, God?

They need an address David says and sends his own.
I try on that hat too.
                Are we twins?
                            we two
whose heads sometimes try not to touch so as not
to read each other's minds or allow the thought
                                        through
and sometimes I spend your dancing money on sweets
but you have plenty plenty and never cry thief.

I try on my grandmother's hat,
                        wide brimmed, trimmed.
She lived a woman's life and I had not thought I had,
but had lived genderless, in pages of books, identifying
with heroes, a mind, unlike a soul, unclothed, do I not talk
to you God, man to man? always thought I did, but longed,
longed and that is female.

                A girl
                    trudging to school
with knees frozen in the wind tunnels of a city,
                                white socks,
skirt, white blouse, I never grudged my dress, my role,
never rebelled, wore the miniskirt I could not manage,
fell off the shoes striding in giant steps, conquering the world,
taking the men I wanted, like a man,
                        earning my living,

like a man, bearing my children, worrying over them,
             worrying them into success,
don't, not like, this, not knowing I was saying
not like me, be a man, or be something.

Should I have said,
                 wash the dishes if they need washing,
know that matriarchy is not just the garden
and finding something to eat, and carrying the load, but
the suddenness of it
from being a school girl, from bare knees, to carrying
what statisticians show to be so great a burden.
                                           Hah!

Ha ha ha!
           Grammie, you laughed so hard
when the painter fell off into the rosebush just after you warned him
that you had to go and hide in the closet,
                               you laughed so hard
when you fell down in the ocean, losing your bearings, laughed so
        hard
to find yourself old and not in control of your body after all
you'd controlled, all the worlds you held up, or
 failed to but were responsible for,
                           like Atlas
dizzy in the waves close to the shore, falling about, and laughing.

Who could have known life
           was so absurd, no, comic, no just plain fine, sun,
water, waves, dizzying splendours that win out at the last?

                                                 God,
look down, see our hats, see how fine we are, and long,
                 long
at long last I know,
                 look at my hat,
I'm a woman after all. Human! Hah!

Tu Fu Speaks

Tu Fu speaks of what is
so it keeps on being so.

The sun on snow,
spears of grass cutting through,
dead in winter.
                        Dead trees
left brutally ragged
by the woodcutter.
                               Time's tricks:
age, loss, death.

Then turning round,
the sudden clearing, the house welcome
as it must have been long ago.

Ancestors

Was it wrong
to leave ancestors behind?
Was it the wrong cry
to send them away?
What should I give
for the solid looks
of their eyes and hands?

I hold to a cup
holding tea, painted flowers
on a table.
Is it the wrong voice
to send it away
floating behind?
Will it ever reach
their firm hands, their red lips?

Family tree

In the books of my life I am alone,
unwilling to see or hear
the band of others who fill up
the morning and move
through the long grasses of midday
and gather together at dusk. But now
let me go down out of the house of myself
and find them there.

*

My father comes into the field at sunset
thinking he's alone, having cast everyone else out
and comes into the field now alone and desolate,
beyond desolate, awakening as if dusk were dawn
and the closing sky an opening one.
At last he is free of the sense of others.
At last he is alone, and can watch the sun
on the water, its vastness, and it is here
on this high hill overlooking the long sparkling waters
that he will build a little house, a house of glass,
emptied of all the demons he's drunk down
and so exorcised from this now innocent glass.

Look how the sunlight catches their wonderful edges
and how together they make a little shelter here
on top of a high hill, as if he were a child here where
the breezes blew gently and bent the grass kindly,
here, where he can wake to the kindly chirping of sparrows,
here he will look down on the waves of grass and sea,
here he will be sheltered in his lovely glass space,
here he will look down from a high hill without
the piercing cries of wind, the demon howlings,
here, far from virtue or vice, here skies illuminate.
Here at last, alone, he hears far away
the sounds of innocent laughter.

*

Up this hill long ago my aunt walked as a young girl
swinging easily along the fence line of this high slope
over the top of the highest piece of land on the Island
with her dear aunt Tad, over the hill and back along
to go to church in Hazelbrook, and back, down the hill
with the wonderful bay stretching far below, and the lovely
trees arching overhead all along the line, and the little
house where Maud lives and watches the birds in summer
and the big house where her grandmother bakes bread and her
Aunt Sadie makes jam out of the tart and lovely grapes
that grow here in the warm shelter of this hill.
And there is grandfather raising his head up from the garden
and raising up his hand, Hello, Hello, we're back.
And it won't matter if years from now her body shrinks down.
It will still walk as far along as to take someone's hand, it
will still remember the sweetness of the way life is.

The aunts

The aunts are far away
walking together under trees
up on a far hill.
I don't know whether
they miss the world
they've given away.
They're wearing hats
under the sun under the trees
picking berries
naming the birds.
Do they wish for the men
or the jobs or the cities they've abandoned?
Not just now.
There's jam to be made.
A dainty striped warbler is calling.
They talk together.
The trees talk in their own way.
The grasses consort.
There's plenty.

Millie

1

where is the stone
for him who lay under the snow?
where is the snow?

time passes,
a moving sidewalk,
everything going
at different speeds,
some of the fallen things
taken aboard,
saved as souvenirs

love lost,
how more lost than by death?
except perhaps
what might never have been
even if they'd all lived,
one dropped here
and one there,
letters left in a shed,
taken up in a tree,
put in order

a house with a red roof,
a cousin's perhaps,
a road that was an address,
random access

the leaves fall
some words remain
arrange them

II

Handsome, young, halfway between sensitive
and cocksure, off in war's great adventure,
he wouldn't have missed it for anything,
seeing all the places they'd read of in the old school,
"and what's keeping some of the rest?
Get out here, don't be lily-livered," he writes home.
This is more excitement than he'd ever have had
if he'd stayed on the Island.

But the Island, and Islanders, is what he thinks of
when he writes to Millie, asking about them,
and telling which ones he meets up with here
in the 105th. "I see Ernest every day.
He's the same old stick and full of mischief."
But, "though there is so many of us here,
it is a very lonesome place." And back home
there is the big race on the 15th, and if only
he had a dozen eggs he'd "tell pretty well then
whether Lauchie had converted or not."
Tell them to buck up and come across he says,
"all the slackers down home," and if he had his way
he'd be over in France sooner than this.

But then, "They don't care what they throw
around here, too much iron for my fancy.
It sure was a hard old time." He's in the hospital,
and she'd heard he was killed, leaving 4 months
without word from her, or home, and what he wrote
was, "Is Jimmie still looking for a wife
or has he found one? And gee, wouldn't I like
to play that trick again on Bob and his buggy.
Do you remember how hard we laughed?"
Dear friend, hoping to be home soon.

III

Home and summer.
Do they meet?
What words they spoke
are not on paper.

The story demands
some resolution
but speakers find more distance
in a few miles than writers in many.

IV

Summer is brief and full on the Island —
hauling the horse, a day with the digger,
Old Home Week, picnics, a tea party,
a big time at Johnnie MacDonald's,
a hen party with Mrs. Chisholm,
jaunts to the Point, and Pinette.

Jessie home from the States,
Florrie from town,
summer romances for Currie and Christie,
Harry and Florrie, Maggie and Dan.
Uncle Willie is home, and Aunt Sarah visits,
Archie MacLean, Florence MacLeod.

Close plantings of friendship,
crowded like flowers, heads of wheat,
the full crop of August, the people of home,
all of them touch and let hands go
joined in a summer's dance,

and Jessie notes she's soon back to Boston,
Ernie to Cambridge,
Harry and Bennie to the camps to cut logs.
Fall, the crop is picked now and the grass
gathered in, and the party disbanded.
There's not many left now.
                              Won't Millie
make up her mind to come too? Her loving cousin.

V

With letters, death is the absence
of words. The end of plans
to meet at church or the picnic,
of sidelong stories about
the rest of us, Maggie and Mary
and Wilfred and Dan, Florence.
Who has gone, and who misses who,
Ha Ha. See you soon.

The cruelty of a clipping.
It's only a few last words.
After an illness of a few days,
Jessie has died in Boston,
age 24, lobar pneumonia.
A few words to make hope
from what can't be believed:
If we are true to ourselves
we shall meet on the shore
where the tree of life blooms
and death is no more.

Here it's lonesome enough
but too common a thing
for more words to crowd on it.

VI

She's busy in her cousin's kitchen,
he in his uncle's fields,
so they only rarely catch a look
and smile a bit awkwardly thinking of all the words
between them, or say some words into the air
and lay them out afterward to dry into meaning.
They lack the right of constant company they'd had apart.
And when he goes to the woods that's when
they can relax into conversation,
dipping a pen in ink, or more often sharpening a pencil
to trace their connection on paper.

VII

Millie's words I know by indirection.
Harry's tell he is not so black as he is painted
nor so green as he is cabbage-looking. There are secrets
he trusts her with and tangles of connections. Secrets
he tells most lovingly, tangled nets he throws over her
to enmesh her who is now his best friend. Bennie sends
his love to my darling pet, my Peggy, ever yours.
XXXX many times, imitations since we are now so far apart.
"You asked why I was so sorry to see you going away.
You never thought I cared so much for you."
But she went, and he went to the logging camps
and then to work at Camp Borden, and the reader despairs.

VIII

The timing might tell.
So when
did Harry steal a kiss
or see how all alone
she was at Willie's
waiting for the mail?
When did Bennie
"keep house" with her
one last not soon forgotten day?
When did he go back to camp?
When did Sarah say,
"Come to Boston with me.
All the crowd is here
And all the good times?"
Who dropped the dice
that scattered all the players
far from the house
with the red roof where the bay
came up on two sides,
or the house on the hill
where the ocean view
was a glimpse far away?

IX

If we pick out the thread of this cloth here is the story
of three friends among dozens. The dance of their interweaving
dips and turns in a sure symmetry, but can we know its fashion?

First. They all like to laugh. Millie carries a thistle.
Bennie turns her upside down. What Harry says is blue.
Second. They leave nobody unscathed and are tarred in turn.

Third. Everybody knows who spoke, laughed, flirted
with who else, but nobody must know who writes to who.
A stolen letter of intimacies makes a good joke, and reveals
what the sheer fabric of openness conceals. "I looked
most innocent and thought you were in Boston,"
says Bennie, "Ever yours, Your pet."

X

It could have been as simple as his getting
a farm in the spring, telling Millie,
"Come home now," but there were delays,
his staying longer at his job, her not getting home
from hers, planning a visit at Christmas
that fell through. He was fascinated by
the excitement of going into the air.
One daredevil took him up, spun in loops
to get the wind up him, but did not.
Men went up, but sometimes
came down faster. One plane you could put
in a basket, though the pilot walked away.
And the work was dangerous, though
he told her not to worry. One day he
came within an inch of losing his head
when the propeller blade started up.
Another time his luck was worse.

XI

Here is the proof he loved:
A. The frequency of his letters.
"I guess I will be raising
the price of writing paper."
B. His vocabulary: "Darling pet,
Sweetheart. Yours ever true."
C. Assurances. "You more than
anything on earth, and it will
always be the same with me."

XII

Who could not love Harry?
Mary, full of his child and bruised
by his resentment, loved him;
Florrie would go away with him;
Dell forgave all; Sarah made lunches
for him; and Millie reassured.
They opened their doors to him.

He loved and thought all loved him,
so perhaps he had no cause to think
of what she might have lost
when he wrote to Millie
just that he'd lost a friend,
"I cried last night to hear such news;
feel awful bad over this sad affair."

With letters, death is the absence of words,
any words to say, I know, to explain,
to say it's all a joke, don't believe it,
to comfort, to answer, to continue.

"I was down to poor Bennie's grave
and his headstone was two feet of snow.
I've heard you were not well, Millie."

No, not well, not well, not well.

XIII

The letters are stricken. They go silent for months,
a year. There is nothing they can say
to Millie, to me, that makes up for this ending.
But they go on, some dozen years, and Millie
herself lives fifty more. It will always be the same
with me, she says perhaps, but packs the letters in a box,
leaving them in a shed one summer she's home. Her friends
find her full of fun and mischief. "Frisky," one calls her.
Another writes, "Hoping to find you as happy a girl
as ever." There is one photo. She and Sarah dancing.

XIV

The tracks in the sand of the blueberry barrens
show that we've picked here, behind the school
at the edge of the gravel pit, in the clean beached boat's shelter,
though we do so discreetly, anxious to avoid accusations of theft
no matter how subtle, or even thoughts in passing cars.

Are they ours, these wild blue fruits ripening in the sun,
a hand's width out of earth, blown by passing breezes
carrying summer's hazy vast sufficiency?

Harry's heirs are gone south, Bennie died young, without,
and Sarah and Millie lived long but passed by in the end,
though their hands filled up kettles of ripe fruit to fill
kitchens with rich treats, and on their stones might read,
as on my grandmother Margaret's, "Where she walked there
flowers grew," as my shoes (Clarks) too leave tracks
of flowers in the dust.
                        Having been here we leave tracks,
tracks on earth, tracks in the wind, tracks on paper,
tracks in each other's thoughts, that grow ripe in summer sun.

Random gifts

I take the random gifts
gratefully, surprised to find

this trove of resurrection
raised up by afternoon brightness,

cascades of lupins in a ditch,
trees that talk without complaint,

air that towers in clouds
whose magnitude and colour,

familiar here, exceed all other airs
in other lands even close by.

And my own people are here,
laid out under stones, name

my family's names and places.
Hedgeways open into houses,

evening lights a door and window,
clipped yards offer me home again.

I call, "Hi Kate, I'm here,"
and listen for the answer.

The Word

God, controversy aside,
is neither an old man nor a girl child,
though in both are carried out
the patterns of force and matter
that shape themselves
in things great and small,
cumulatively one plasma, this universe,
micromessage and manifestation, the Word.

And where are we? We stand
under the stars, we stand
by the sea, we stand on the red
earth of this island. In our blood
atoms and planets reproduce themselves,
living out their miraculous and similar destinies.

If we could stand so, still,
we would be eternal as God.
But somehow, our hearts bite,
we do, strike, we are awake.
The trees shake in the vulnerable air.
The very mantle of the earth meets
and overtakes itself, somewhere.

When earth goes underground
new mountains quake.
When trees fell, worms
make nurseries for some new life
to break into the ether,
breathing our delicate chains of gases.

Even without all this
rocks would hurtle through space,
burn and revolve. But we love
our drops of air and life,
our small and infinite designs.
We love the touch of flesh, the grit of sand,
clouds arching across a clear sky.

The dying of trees

The earth is waiting
for its ice age.

As to a child
feverishly playing at bedtime
sleep restores,
so ice grinds as dust
over an era tired out by excess,

recedes to leave new energies
for outbursts of trees
and the birds and songs
and lumbering or darting forms
life takes in them
growing, devouring, dying,
soaking in sun,
waves of meadowflowers
waves of cloud overhead
whispering of leaves.

And then, quick or slow,
the rock dust pulls under,
the trees weaken their hold,
life weakens its hold,
it gets quiet.
The ice thinks of dropping down
to cover the eyes.

Child or old man,
everyone needs rest.
When the energy's used,
when the trees are gone,
then it's time for the soothing
cool hand of ice
to comfort the stone.

November Gregorian

white house lit in a violet sky
white berries hung on dry branches
the smooth Gregorian exploding
into nasal alternate saxophones
a trumpeting of termination

to live November is to be alone
in the great company of the undone
to be on the turning down of the wheel
voices singing round a single note
of hold, hold, and go down in black night

and bury in the dark
and if God wills it
come up spring and morning

Random words — *pax*

How strange opening the book
to find so many words
of joy, of dawn, of hope,
of praise, of God.

Leaving God *out* of poems
has become my mission,
to keep one word from turning
the tide from fact.

To avoid skipping a page
saying God, power, wisdom, intent
is at work and not as it seems
too many, too late, too needy.

Overfishing, ozone, rainforest, loss,
war, AIDS, a litany of our defeats.
Balance them against home, love,
landscape, tell the truth.

But what do these random words
speak of but praise, soul, genius,
bliss, the song of songs, the voice
of God walking in the garden?

Bliss was it in that dawn
Our birth is a sleep and a forgetting
In a better world than this
All men naturally desire to know.

All is, has been, will be, God,
bliss, knowledge, dream, peace,
possible, quiet, lovely.
Then praise God, oh my soul.

Aura

The first time I had my aura read
was at Ellie's where she told how
much fun they'd had at a party, and now
she could see auras around everyone's head.

And mine? I asked. She studied the air
around me and said, I can't really tell about you.
Which I took to mean that no aura was clear
and if I had one it must be the grey of fog or dew.

Not much room for vanity there,
but then another time a man came up to me
and said he could see fireworks of every degree
and colour shooting out of me everywhere.

He said it was the brightest aura he'd seen
and what did I think about it? What did it mean?
I didn't know what to say, even though I knew
that what he said was something quite true:

it was something I sometimes feel and remember
feeling just then and having to pause for,
while the flames around my head died to an ember,
wondering whether my hair was standing up or

my face turned red or what it looks like
from the outside when the current of my life
reaches out to touch the current of God,
suddenly near and no smaller, but in touch:

that friendship, recognition, mingling of matter
that you know sometimes when you're driving the car
and are amazed at how beautiful the thing is near and far
and say, Thanks God, and then the energy flutters

out of your head, and the wings of your energy beat
in some suddenly large scale and join
with the green of earth pushing out of brown
and the air where the water of the bay and the clouds meet

and there you are, joined in some electric current
that sweeps in as far as the ocean comes in
and as high as to meet aurora borealis when
the sky shakes across the night in green curtains

and it's all as delicate and natural as life
is at its best when all your blood is flowing in your veins
and everything's calm and alive and working right
and you are you but attached to everything wonderful and strange

and flowing and moving and still centred in one spot
which is attached to everything else and not
pulling or pushing but floating and flying on the air
and knowing and loving and moving everywhere.

It isn't the everyday thing for anyone, including me,
but that's what an aura is, just electricity
that touches electricity, and when you know what it is
you like to have the grey cloak off sometimes and sizzle.

The path

A long walk, circular, ending at home,
damp, I don't mind damp, slanting rain,
the circularity of journeys, of life,
sitting in a warm bed, reading poetry,
finding a pen, no, I don't mind.

Yes, I was lost awhile on this walk, the same
with life, that's alright, I'm here now,
my pants are hanging on the back of a chair
beside the heating vent. Just as we walked
the last steps, Jessie lagging, and me
turning round to check on her, the car stopped,
David had come looking, and we got in.

In the woods, walking on moss, following trails
that led farther and farther away, walking on damp moss,
I thought how sweet it would be to lie down on it
some day, the last day, with a blanket and a book,
and several pens in a plastic bag, to savour
the going, the wind in the trees, the damp moss,
the way time passed, the way it was no longer important
to get up, and how I would record it.

Some strange moment in the telling I would make then
of David finding me there and lying down
to watch awhile; delusion, or not,
perhaps he would find me, wouldn't betray me,
would come, one last time, to lie beside me.

It's deep and green here, a wood place, wood paths,
the sound of woods, and in one spot, a concourse
of birds, how far we must be from everything!
And no, I have not kept track and don't know
which way is forward or which back, roads fork,
there is no end of woods or roads, but at last
a rooftop over a field, a house on a river,
a road at the end of a lane, a long mud road,
the highway at last, which will certainly go home,
but the longest part's the measured road, the known.

The Author

Judy Gaudet was born in Prince Edward Island. She now lives in Belfast, PEI, with her partner, David Helwig, and works as a teacher and librarian in Charlottetown. Judy grew up in Montreal, and was educated at Bishop's and Queen's Universities. She has three grown daughters: Mary, Caitlin, and Christina. *Her Teeth Are Stones* is her first book of poetry.

Some of these poems have previously appeared in *blueSHIFT*, *The Gaspereau Review*, and *ContemporaryVerse2*, as well as in the anthologies *A Bountiful Harvest*, *Landmarks*, and *The Poets of Prince Edward Island*, and have been broadcast on CBC Radio as part of the Live Poets Society broadcast. Saturday Morning Chapbooks published *Poems, you say* in 2003.